SELLING

> Buying Decisions Are Not Made on Golf Courses, Restaurants, Trade-Show Floors, Kitchen Tables, or Buying Offices, But in the Mind of the Buyer.

IS A
MIND GAME

Warren Schoening

authorHOUSE®

AuthorHouse™
1663 Liberty Drive
Bloomington, IN 47403
www.authorhouse.com
Phone: 1-800-839-8640

© 2012 by Warren Schoening. All rights reserved.

No part of this book may be reproduced, stored in a retrieval system, or transmitted by any means without the written permission of the author.

Published by AuthorHouse   02/09/2012

ISBN: 978-1-4685-4593-7 (sc)
ISBN: 978-1-4685-4592-0 (hc)
ISBN: 978-1-4685-4594-4 (ebk)

Library of Congress Control Number: 2012901175

Any people depicted in stock imagery provided by Thinkstock are models, and such images are being used for illustrative purposes only.
Certain stock imagery © Thinkstock.

This book is printed on acid-free paper.

Because of the dynamic nature of the Internet, any web addresses or links contained in this book may have changed since publication and may no longer be valid. The views expressed in this work are solely those of the author and do not necessarily reflect the views of the publisher, and the publisher hereby disclaims any responsibility for them.

CONTENTS

ACKNOWLEDGMENTS vii
INTRODUCTION ix
UNDERSTANDING THE GAME 1
    THE ART OF PERSUASION 3
    TAKING THE SALES STAGE 7
    ETHICS 9
    SALES CONVERSATION 11
    SELLING LANDSCAPE 15
MEETING OF THE MINDS 23
    BUYER'S MENTAL PROCESS 25
    DISCIPLINES OF SELLING 29
    CONNECTING 31
    OPENING 37
    PROPOSAL 43
    FEATURES & BENEFITS 47
    PROOF SOURCE 55
    BUYING SIGNALS 59
    CLOSE 63
    CLOSING TECHNIQUES 65
WHEN MINDS DON'T MEET 77
    OBJECTIONS 79
    WHY BUYERSPRESENT OBJECTIONS 87
    HANDLING OBJECTIONS CHECK LIST 89
    HANDLING OBJECTION TECHNIQUES 91

COMMITMENT	105
YOUR DECISION	107
ABOUT THE AUTHOR	111

ACKNOWLEDGMENTS

All the blessings in my life have been provided by my savior and lord Jesus Christ.

Heartfelt love and thanks to my beloved wife, Karen, who stood by my side from my first field sales position and through multiple relocations as I dragged her and our much-loved sons Brian and Jeremy across the country.

A collective thanks to all the buyers and clients I've called on over the years for their real-life lessons. These sales encounters did more to assist me in accruing selling skills than any other venue. A special thanks to those who were not only business acquaintances but became real friends.

Also, thanks to all who gave me a chance and believed in me enough to advance my career.

INTRODUCTION

Sales is really the world's oldest profession. Nothing transpires until someone offers to sell and another decides to buy, exchanging acceptable value for product rendered or received.

In this book, the word *product* refers to tangible or intangible items to be sold, including goods, services, financial instruments, insurance, real estate, and contracts.

It is amazing the number of individual salespeople whose performance falls far short of their clients' or their company's expectations. This lack of skill inhibits the chances for sales success, promotion, increased income, and even continued employment.

Skilled salespeople are not born—they're developed. Natural talent and personality provide a basis for considering sales as a profession. However, the winning ingredients are a desire to achieve, self-discipline, and self-motivation. For those who will commit to personal skill development, the world of sales provides an exciting, challenging, and rewarding career.

In today's environment of rapid information exchange, sound-bite communication, text messaging, and exploding technology, selling requires a fully stocked toolbox. *Selling Is a Mind Game* can help you put one together. It's a comprehensive guide for individuals who are entering the sales profession, or for the veteran to re-examine basic sales fundamentals' for successful selling. The information is presented in a straightforward manner for a quick read, with content focusing on the buyer's mental process and the interaction between buyer and seller, as well as sales disciplines, techniques, and additional skills necessary for success.

It is impossible to address every industry or individual situation with specific examples. An expansive approach for conceptual understanding provides each reader the opportunity to apply individual product and industry knowledge for personal skill development.

It's important for each individual to find the right industry and product to sell. The industry should be one the individual believes in, and the product should perform as advertised. When seeking employment, research potential companies and consider only those whose integrity and reputation have value in their industry.

Being in the right industry with the right product provides self-esteem, confidence when conversing with family, friends, and business associates, and most important, conviction when selling to clients.

UNDERSTANDING THE GAME

HOW THE PIECES FIT

THE ART OF PERSUASION

THE ART OF PERSUASION

Wikipedia Encyclopedia defines persuasion as "a form of social influence. It is the process of guiding people and oneself toward the adoption of an idea, attitude, or action by rational and symbolic means."

At its most basic, selling is the ability to influence others and gain acceptance of the proposition you are putting forth.

Selling is a people business. Individuals are more likely to be persuaded by those they like and feel comfortable with. However, although having a rapport or a personal friendship with a prospective client may provide a meeting and selling opportunity, it will not close the sale.

Decisions are not made on golf courses, restaurants, trade-show floors, kitchen tables, or even buying offices.

DECISION-MAKING IS A MENTAL PROCESS
SELLING IS A MIND GAME

The Art of Persuasion:

- Requires an understanding of the buyer's mental position, which is molded by personal bias, motivations, personality, job demands, attitudes, belief system, cultural background, hobbies, education, and how his or her personal life maybe going on any given day.

- Requires reasoning with the buyer using logic, providing essential benefits, proof of performance, rhetoric, presentation material, facts, figures, charts, graphs, and third-party testimonial support.

- Requires appealing to buyer's emotions—using belief system, tradition, social pressures, and fears as touchstones, and touting benefits and gratification from company perks, bonuses, or vendor rewards.

- Requires selling skills, handling objections, verbal and written communication, conflict management, and body language.

Despite all of the effort expended in producing the perfect proposal material, too many salespeople forget to factor in the buyer's mental position. Your must identify that position before starting to sell. Consider:

- What specific benefits are required by the buyer?

- What are the individual's personal motivational factors?

- Is the buyer a numbers person who makes decisions "based on the story the numbers tell"?

- Is the buyer a visual learner, who prefers to get information from charts & graphs?

- Does the buyer make decisions based on emotion?

- Does the buyer have strong personal opinions regarding the proposed product or service?

- Is there potential for cultural background and experiences to influence the decision-making process?

- What objections could the buyer present?

- Is the buyer authorized to make a buying decision, or will other people be participating buying process?

A sales conversation with seller and buyer on the same mental track provides a ticket on the train to sales success.

TAKING THE SALES STAGE

What's the difference between an average salesperson and a sales superstar? What's the difference between a talented singer and a rock star? Stage presence, showmanship, and an ability to captivate the audience separates the run-of-the-mill form the elite.

Salespeople are the principal performers on the sales stage.

As a teenager, I attended a home show in south Texas on a fall afternoon with some friends. Walking down the aisle, we scanned the booths in an effort to identify cool new products. Slightly behind us on our left came an unexpected, enthusiastic voice bellowing out, "Want to stretch your dollars?" My involuntary human reaction kicked in, and I along with others in the aisle turned to see who was posing such a question. There he was, holding a dollar bill at each end in front of him so everyone could see it. In one quick motion, the rubber dollar bill was stretched several times across his chest as far as of both arms would reach, followed by "Step closer and learn how to stretch your dollars!" The crowd moved closer, the sales pitch (performance) was given, and product was sold. I don't remember *what* was being sold, but I still recall how my attention was captured. On that day, I learned that gaining attention and interest is a prerequisite to selling a product.

Without the core competencies of product knowledge and selling skills, your efforts will fall short. However loaded as you may be with product knowledge, without "stage presence," the client (audience) maybe left flat and unmotivated.

From the initial client greeting, a salesperson is onstage, performing with each presentation delivered. The practiced ability to deliver a persuasive message cannot be underestimated. Extraordinary success combines knowledge, selling skills, and stage presence.

Delivering a presentation is performing for the buyer. Salespeople have a license to develop a stage presence or persona that allows for exceptional behavior. When taking the sales stage, carefully consider the client and target the benefits he or she desires. All clients are unique, and each may require a different approach. Don't become a one-role actor. Selling a dream vacation on a cruise ship going to an exotic island requires a different approach than selling funeral services.

During the sales encounter, exhibit self-confidence, appropriate voice inflection, product knowledge, enthusiasm, positive body language, command of the presentation, and a strong conviction that the product will perform as advertised.

A strong performance on the sales stage will seize attention, gain the interest of your buyers, and improve your closing percentage.

ETHICS

A salesperson's most valuable assists are name and reputation. Your personal and professional integrity must meet the highest standard of individual and business ethics.

All industries are small, regardless of dollar volume. Salespeople are known by their personal and business activities. The way a salesperson conducts business will determine both short-and long-term success and failure.

Developing a strong track record of honest, up-front ethical business dealings pays dividends in client confidence, respect, and a willingness to do business. A reputation for integrity maintains current clients on board and assists you in gaining new ones.

Early in my career, I attended a sales meeting introducing a new product designed to compete with a competitive product already entrenched with solid market share. A high priority had been placed on wide-scale acceptance and distribution. I asked the vice president of sales about the boundaries and latitudes the sales group was to operate under in achieving our sales objectives. The response was, "Don't do anything immoral or illegal. Everything else is fair."

If you are ever in doubt regarding ethical selling and business dealings, simply remember the issues of morality and legality, and your name and reputation will not be tarnished.

DON'T DO ANYTHING IMMORAL OR ILLEGAL
EVERYTHING ELSE IS FAIR

SALES CONVERSATION

Salespeople speaking 75 percent of the time during a sales proposal are not engaged in a conversation—but a one-way dialogue boring to the buyer and, in many cases, leaving the buyer skeptical and not excited to buy. People want to have a conversation, not to be talked at. The best route to making a sale is gaining buyer participation in a conversation.

Sales conversations require both buyer and seller to engage in a two-way exchange and interact in open communication. The dialogue is to be probing, honest, relaxed, and non-threatening, with both parties receiving and providing information. Keep it interesting and entertaining if possible. Provide product benefits and solve problems at both the business and personal level for the buyer.

Listening skills are required for an effective conversation. At times, salespeople are too busy talking—trying to sell—that they don't listen to the client. It is important to determine how information is being processed by the client and how best to proceed. Active listening means hearing and analyzing what is actually being communicated so that important selling clues are not missed. Salespeople who dominate the conversation experience a lower closing rate, as they have not learned what is important to the client. A conscious effort must be made to keep the dialogue open, with important issues unearthed and addressed.

Formal presentation material (facts, figures, charts, graphs, third—party support) is used to direct, control, and support the selling objective. Information received or provided by buyer and seller become discussion points. These major decision-making issues should be reviewed through a brief exchange to assure agreement or uncover an objection. Merely providing information will not convince the buyer that the product is worth purchasing.

Proposals are to be persuasive, providing benefits that are readily understood making it easy for the buyer to say yes.

Trust between the buyer and seller is paramount in gaining the first sale and developing an ongoing sales relationship. Trust cannot be obtained by making presentations; it requires a conversation, using solid communication skills in answering questions asked and unasked. Through buyer involvement and participation, interest is developed and confidence in the seller is established.

As important as dialogue is, it's also important to *stop selling* upon receiving an affirmative buying response.

As a teenage salesperson working at a discount store selling televisions, I greeted a customer who pointed out a top-of-the—line TV and said, "I want to buy that one."

Excited and eager for the sale, I replied, "Great choice! Let me tell you about that set."

The customer quickly responded, "I am on my lunch break, and don't have time for a sales pitch. Write it up now or I'm leaving."

Don't be an "un-closer" by continuing to "sell" bringing up irrelevant, extraneous, or unwanted information that may cultivate a concern or objection. Don't talk yourself out of a sale! Move to the next step: finalize the sale, write the order, sign a contract.

SELLING LANDSCAPE

Each baseball season starts at spring training, with players focusing on conditioning, practice, and execution of the basics. Players and managers know these make the difference for a winning season.

Professional athletes are individuals with God-given physical talent that cannot be duplicated, regardless of how hard one tries. In sales, there are a few "natural" salespeople, but unlike athletes, special physical talent is not required. Mental strength, however, is essential. The majority of professional salespeople are not "born" but attain knowledge and develop personal selling skills that lead to superior performance.

An understanding of the field or landscape salespeople play on every day is essential in ascertaining how the game is to be played. Pitcher and batter, seller and buyer—all strive to reach personal objectives. Sellers' objectives are servicing accounts and closing sales, while buyers are looking to meet corporate or personal objectives.

In the 1950s, my dad farmed in south Texas and planted acres of tomatoes, as did other farmers that season. With no government regulation or crop subsidies, there was a glut of tomatoes on the open market, and he was unable to sell his crop.

To raise money for the family, large brown paper "barrel" bags were purchased at the local grocery store and filled with tomatoes handpicked from the field. I got my first selling lesson as a young boy selling tomatoes door to door. Being quite young and not having any selling experience, I learned several valuable lessons:

- The key to selling is asking someone to buy.

- The more contacts I made, the more I sold.

- Not everyone will buy.

- Don't take rejection personally.

Though I didn't know it at the time, this was also my first lesson in developing an understanding of the "Rule of 80."

RULE OF 80

80 PERCENT WILL BUY *IF SOLD*
10 PERCENT WILL BUY *IF ASKED*
10 PERCENT MAY NEVER BUY

Future selling encounters provided lessons, cementing the need and importance for developing personal selling skills. In addition, I learned about the selling field landscape.

LANDSCAPE RULE # 1
Buyers are the gatekeepers, determining the success of a salesperson based on buying decisions, positive or negative.

Just as sales personnel attend sales training seminars, many corporate buyers attend training seminars on how to leverage their position in the buying and selling process. Buyers' decisions hinge on their opinion of what is in the best interest of the company or themselves personally. Closings skyrocket when sought-after company benefits and personal buyer benefits are provided simultaneously.

Personal relationships between buyer and seller may get you an appointment, but appointments do not guarantee sales success.

Success depends on the seller's skills in persuading the buyer to open the buying gate.

LANDSCAPE RULE # 2
Sellers must be able to sell "friendlies" because "non-friendlies" won't buy.

Competitive products being equal, the Rule of 80 suggests that 10 percent of buyers will purchase if simply asked to buy, need the product or service, like the seller, or like the seller's company. Meanwhile, 10 percent may never buy, choosing not to do business because they dislikes the seller, dislikes the seller's company, or have a friend or family member selling a similar competitive product or service.

Landscape Rule # 3
Sales success comes from the 80 percent who will buy if sold—the Rule of 80.

The mark of a professional salesperson is the ability to gain a high close rate within the 80 percent of those who will buy if *sold*. Let there be no doubt that career success and financial reward are produced by this 80 percent. A salesperson must understand that selling is a process requiring in-depth knowledge and artful execution of selling disciplines and techniques to succeed.

Landscape Rule # 4
Set yourself apart from the competition.

There may be one or several competitors vying for the same business and providing similar benefits. What separates the herd of salespeople from a professional salesperson? Set yourself apart, connect with the buyer on a personal level as an individual, understand what the buyer provides as information, make your word your bond, provide value, respect others, and be an expert in product and industry knowledge who is willing to go the extra mile when necessary.

Buyers evaluate sellers and prefer to do business with those they relate to and feel confident in. Relationships built on the aforementioned traits will provide long-term sales success and keep the competition on the outside looking in.

Landscape Rule # 5
Establish sales-call objectives.

Without defined sales-calls objectives, salespeople are just well-paid tourists leaving results to happenstance. Determine primary and secondary objectives for each sales call. Once objectives are established, initiate pre-call work-gathering information to determine what is important to the buyer both professionally and personally. Develop sales material parallel to the buyer's mental process, focusing on sales-call objectives.

Landscape Rule # 6
Follow-up, follow-up, follow-up! Presentence pays.

Stay in communication. Follow-up each sales call with a secondary sales visit, recap letter, e-mail, phone, or fax.

If you are unable to close the sale during the initial sales call, follow-up contact is required. Prior to exiting the initial sales call, schedule another face-to-face meeting. If a face-to-face follow-up is unattainable, establish a phone follow-up appointment, including day, date, and time. When contacting the buyer at the established time, remind them of the appointment or phone follow-up that was established at the conclusion of the prior meeting. If the buyer has not made a decision at the conclusion of the follow-up contact, determine the major objections and establish another face-to-face sales call or specific phone-appointment follow-up.

Upon receiving an order from a follow-up, insure that it is processed accurately, meeting all requirements agreed upon by the buyer and seller.

As a salesperson for a wholesale distributor selling to independent retail grocery stores, gaining new accounts was part of my sales responsibility. Cold-calling on an opportunity account, I identified Dave as the person of authority, presented myself, and announced the company I represented. Unknown to me, Dave had a prior unpleasant experience with the company, and before I knew what was happening my sales bag was pitched out the door, sliding across the sidewalk and into the gutter. Looking at my sales bag and then back at Dave, I said, "What's the deal? I might be a nice guy."

With an embarrassed look, he responded, "You're right, I am sorry, but just to let you know, I hate your company and will never do business with you."

I accepted the apology and asked if it would be a problem if I called on him from time to time. He said okay but reiterated that he would never buy from the company I represented.

I continued to call on Dave for several months, developing a personal relationship. However, our business relationship had not grown into a single sales dollar. The week prior to a major national holiday, I called on Dave and identified that he was out—of—stock on an item that was the most popular in its category. I suggested he purchase the item from me. He said no. I pointed out the lost dollars and unhappy customers this condition would produce. I proposed to solve this costly problem, and he would not have to continue to buy from my company in the future. Considering the position he was in, Dave agreed to take advantage of this offer.

Within six months following the first order, my company was shipping 50 percent of his everyday business.

Follow-up ~ Follow-up ~ Follow-up ~ Presentence Pays

LANDSCAPE RULE # 7
Mental Toolbox

Electricians, plumbers, mechanics, dentists, and doctors all have toolboxes containing an array of tools and instruments to be used for a specific application. Salespeople carry their tools of the trade—such as selling skills and ability to handle objections—in their mind or "mental toolbox." Sales success is based on the degree to which the mental toolbox is stocked (knowledge) and the ability (skill level) to select and utilize the required tools (techniques) in persuading buyers.

LANDSCAPE RULE # 8
Obtaining selling skills is an individual responsibility.

Professional sales seminar trainers indicate that only 10 to 15 percent of seminar attendees will learn what was taught and put it into practice in the field. Jump in front of that "herd" of salespeople. There are self-help sales books, CDs, sales seminars, supervisors teaching and coaching, and just plain learning as one goes. ***It's your career—invest in yourself.***

MEETING OF THE MINDS

INCREASED SALES IS THE REWARD FOR BEING PREPARED

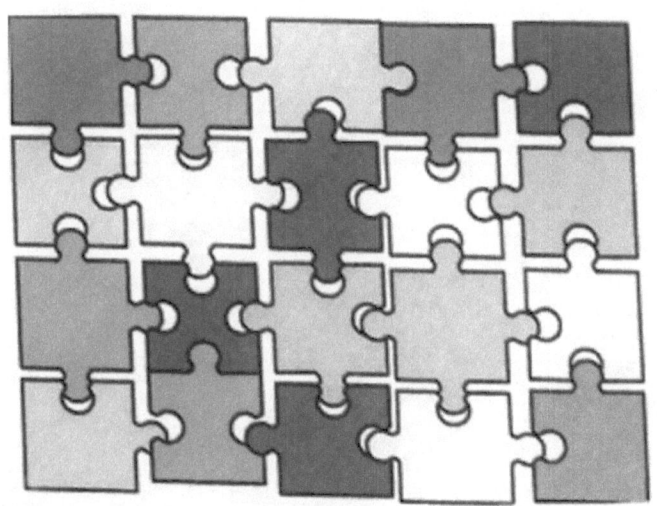

FAILURE IS THE PENALTY FOR A LACK OF PREPAREDNESS

BUYER'S MENTAL PROCESS

Effective selling requires an understanding of how buyers think—their mental process when making a buying decision. Understanding this process is important, as it is the key to developing a successful sales conversation. Generally, the buyer's initial mindset is that of *indifference* and is usually at a "zero-float"—neither for or against what is about to be propose. The salesperson must create *interest* and involvement to earn the right to continue on to the proposal. Buyers process and *evaluate* proposal information, and a *decision* is made that leads to the final position of *action*. Only then will the buyer accept or reject the proposal.

A favorable setting and relaxed atmosphere are desirable—however, buying decisions are not made on the golf course, in restaurants, or at offices, but made in the buyer's mind. Sales conversations and presentation material must parallel the way buyers mentally process information.

BUYER'S MENTAL PROCESS

INDIFFERENT
THE BUYER
DOES NOT FEEL POSITIVE OR NEGATIVE

PROPOSAL EVALUATION
THE BUYER
PROCESS PROPOSAL INFORMATION,
CONSIDERS PRODUCT OR PROGRAM BENEFITS

DECISION
THE BUYER
DETERMINES VALUE OF
PRODUCT OR PROGRAM VERSES RISK

ACTION
THE BUYER
ACCEPT OR REJECT PROPOSAL
COMMUNICATES DECISION

Buyer indifference is not negative, but a reflection of not having developed a position on what is being presented. Generally, this is due to insufficient information (new product, concepts) or misinformation regarding the existing product.

Sellers must gain buyer interest and attention. If the buyer isn't interested, little mental effort will be invested in processing proposal information. It will go in one ear and out the other.

Proposals must provide relative value—features and benefits—pertaining to products being offered. Value, real or perceived, provides the greatest opportunity for persuading the buyer and gaining a sale. After receiving proposal information, the buyer moves to the next step in the natural thought sequence and formulates an opinion, positive or negative. He or she may request additional information that could impact the decision. After all information is processed, the buyer finally makes a decision and moves into action mode, communicating that decision to the seller.

All of us are buyers. As individuals, our mental process is identical to that of professional buyers or individual consumer clients. Consider how you mentally process information when confronted with a buying decision.

Early one evening, while you are watching TV, the doorbell rings. You open the door, and there stands a young person. "Hi, my name is Taylor."

Being *indifferent*, you provide a courteous response. "How may I help you?"

Taylor replies, "I deliver the Metro Times Newspaper. Would you like to buy a subscription?"

You take a few seconds for *evaluating*. You don't have time to read a newspaper everyday. You receive plenty of news from the Internet, TV, and radio. With these factors in mind, you move to *decision* making. Not perceiving any real benefits or value, decide that you have no interest. You then move into *action* responding, "No thanks, not today," declining the proposal.

Although this is a simple example, we all have experienced a similar situation. As individual consumers, we follow the same mental path as professional buyers: *indifferent, evaluation, decision,* and *action.*

It goes without saying, the greater the impact of a buying decision, the more extensive the consideration and evaluation of the proposal's benefits and value will be prior to making a decision or taking action.

LANDSCAPE RULE # 1
Buyers are the gatekeepers, determining the success of a salesperson based on their buying decisions, positive or negative.

LANDSCAPE RULE # 3
Sales success comes from the 80 percent that will buy if sold—the Rule of 80.

DISCIPLINES OF SELLING

Selling disciplines are designed to coincide with the buyer's natural mental process when evaluating information and making a buying decision.

DISCIPLINE	OBJECTIVE
Connecting	INITIATE A BRIEF PERSONAL CONVERSATION DEVELOPING COMMON GROUND, LEADING THE BUYER TO VIEW YOU AS AN INDIVIDUAL RATHER THAN JUST ANOTHER SALESPERSON.
Opening	OVERCOME INDIFFERENCE, GAIN BUYER'S INTEREST, INVOLVE THE BUYER, AND EARN THE RIGHT TO CONTINUE ON TO THE PROPOSAL.
Proposal	MAINTAIN INTEREST, OBTAIN BUYER PARTICIPATION, PROVIDE VALUE, AND GAIN CONVICTION.
Close	A CALL FOR POSITIVE ACTION.

Disciplines apply to almost all activities. For example, to drive an automobile, the first requirement is unlocking the door, followed by getting in, inserting the key into the ignition, starting the engine, engaging the gear, and pressing on the accelerator. These are driving disciplines that must be completed to move the car forward.

Like driving, selling has disciplines that must be successfully completed to move a sale forward. Each selling discipline has a specific objective and is aligned with the buyer's mental process, steering the proposal toward a positive buying decision. If any discipline is missed, the likelihood of success is reduced.

It is important to note that each salesperson is an individual with a personality influencing the manner or style in which proposals will be delivered. Disciplines of selling should not be confused with style, as each is distinctly unique and different.

Sellers must be comfortable with the material being presented and confident in their selling skills and individual presentation style when taking the sales stage. Personal selling style should not be altered but integrated with selling disciplines.

SELLING DISCIPLINES ARE THE PROCESS
STYLE IS AN INDIVIDUAL'S SELLING PERSONALITY

LANDSCAPE RULE # 7
Mental Toolbox

CONNECTING

By design, the buyer's position is to buy and the seller's position is to sell. All too often, this is seen as adversarial, placing buyer and seller at opposite sides of the table. The objective of connecting is to quickly establish a personal connection, with the buyer seeing you as an individual rather than just another salesperson.

To connect with the buyer, initiate a short, friendly, personal—that is, nonbusiness—conversation based on common ground or interests. This produces a relaxed atmosphere and reduces barriers of suspicion, skepticism, and initial resistance.

As a sales manager traveling the country from sea to shining sea, it was my business practice to wear a suite and tie. One late fall afternoon, I was accompanied by a local sales associate who dressed in the local custom. We stopped in on a small wholesale distributor in the bayou country of Louisiana.

As we entered the buyer's office, he looked directly at me and without hesitation stated, "I don't buy anything from slick salespeople wearing suites and ties."

Realizing he wasn't joking, I asked, "Do you know why I'm wearing a suit and tie?"

Taking a second, he responded, "No."

I replied, "I call on accounts from New York to Los Angeles that require me to wear a suit and tie, and I would show you no less respect than I do for other buyers I call on."

He took a deep breath, leaned back in his chair, and said, "Take that tie off and tell me why you're here."

Connect with the buyer as a person. The amount of information that can be harvested is amazing. A better understanding in conducting business at both the individual and company level will pay huge dividends.

All too often, salespeople try to connect using conversation topic areas they are comfortable with rather than determining where the buyer's interest lie. Sports seem to be the salesperson's universal subject of choice, but that's impersonal and focuses on teams or individual players, not on the buyer.

There is nothing wrong with sports as a topic if the buyer is truly interested; however, generally the conversation provides little knowledge of interests or personal insight into the buyer. People like to talk about themselves and important or interesting events in their lives. Lead your buyer into doing just that. This is the time to listen and learn. Focus on connecting conversations on these areas of interest or importance.

Connecting conversations must be honest and sincere. Anything less will produce a negative attitude that will affect the buyer's acceptance of you personally and of your proposal. During the conversation, the buyer also has the opportunity to gain information about you. Consciously or unconsciously, buyers develop attitudes and feelings towards sellers, and these form the foundation of the buy/sell relationship.

Prior to a sales trip to the Pacific Rim, I was advised by my sales manager not to discuss business until a willingness to do so was indicated by the buyer. Local custom and culture required buyers to evaluate salespeople prior to doing business. Fifteen minutes of conservation passed before the buyer indicated it was time to move on to the business portion of the appointment.

Some salespeople may have a concern for time spent in the connecting discipline and the impact on total time that may be allotted by the buyer for the sales call. Concern in some cases maybe justified and may not allow for spending much time in this discipline; however, most buyers will provide additional time as long as the connecting and proposal conversations are interesting to them. Have you ever spent time in a waiting area far past your designated appointment time? Well, some salesperson captured the buyer's interest and exceeded his or her allotted time—only to use yours.

Making it interesting and getting the buyer involved are the keys to connecting with the buyer on a personal level. Consider these sources for connecting topics.

INFORMATION SOURCES	CONNECTING TOPIC AREAS
Surroundings ~~~~	LOOK FOR PICTURES OF FAMILY, DIPLOMAS, SPECIAL RECOGNITION AWARDS, INTERESTING ITEMS, GENERAL OFFICE CONDITION.
Personal Attributes ~~~~~~	NOTICE THE BUYER'S NAME, SPEECH, ACCENT, CLOTHING, JEWELRY, AGE. IS THERE SOMETHING YOU CAN COMPLIMENT?
Buyer History ~~~	HOW LONG WITH THE COMPANY? HOW LONG AS A BUYER? HOW LONG BUYING THE PRODUCT OR SERVICE BEING PRESENTED?

Personal clues are abundant on walls, desks, and other surrounding areas in offices or in the home. Individuals themselves provide a wealth of topic areas for interesting and informative conversation. Don't overlook clues like attire, surnames, accent, and age as they relate to individual characteristics, personality, and experience.

Additionally, conversation can provide insight into the buyer's attitude and views toward the company, allowing you to develop a better understand of company guidelines for doing business.

Develop open-ended questions for initiating conversations focused on topics that will provide insight into personal information, interests, and personality. Questions must be genuine, not patronizing, and conveyed in a sincere manner.

It is essential to be a good listener. The buyer is invited to open up in conversation, and this is your time to listen. If personal opinions differ, do not argue; shift the conversation to an alternative topic area.

When in the connecting discipline, always let the buyer be the authority on the topic being discussed. The same courtesy will be extended to you when you're presenting your proposal.

Landscape Rule # 2
Sellers must be able to sell "friendlies," as "non-friendlies" won't buy.

Landscape Rule # 4
Set yourself apart from the competition.

OPENING

The opening discipline is the cornerstone of an effective sales conversation. Its *only* objective is to gain the buyer's interest and earn the right to continue on to the proposal. Interest level and involvement, be it positive or negative, will be determined at this point of the sales encounter. Subsequent interaction throughout the selling process hinges on an effective opening.

OPENING DISCIPLINES

Brief

5-15 SECONDS

Five to fifteen seconds is all you need. The objective is to capture the buyer's attention and interest as quickly as possible. We live in a sound-bite world in which less is more. Don't confuse the buyer with a long opening dissertation. This is not your proposal.

Word Selection

CHOOSE WORDS THAT
ARE SALES OBJECTIVE ORIENTED

Choose words that are sales-objective oriented. Word selection supporting the objective is critical, as it provides a positive path, avoids confusion, and focuses attention on the sales objective. Additionally, word selection should provide a natural transition into the proposal.

Create Interest

OVERCOME INDIFFERENCE

Your opening should be aimed at overcoming any indifference the buyer may feel. Utilize provocative opening questions or statements to peak interest. Sellers must earn the right to continue on to the proposal segment, with buyers interested in learning more. Without interest, little attention will be given to the message contained within the proposal.

Engage

GAIN THE BUYERS PARTICIPATION

Its human nature—people dislike being talked at. They prefer to participate in a conversation. Now is the time to get the buyer involved in the sales conversation. Asking a question requiring a response, making a provocative statement, or using the buyer's senses will engage him or her in open dialogue regarding the product or services being proposed.

Landscape Rule # 1
Buyers are the gatekeepers, determining the success of a salesperson based on their buying decisions, positive or negative.

Landscape Rule # 4
Set yourself apart from the competition

OPENING TECHNIQUES

> *Question* ~~~~ **DEVELOP QUESTIONS THAT GENERATE INTEREST AND REQUIRES A RESPONSE FROM THE BUYER.**

Questions must be carefully framed with word selection to support the selling objective, stimulate interest, and spur the buyer to respond in a predetermined manner. In other words, *know the answer to the question before asking.*

Generally, in the opening discipline (as opposed to connecting), closed-ended questions requiring only a yes or no response are preferred—for example, "Would you like to cut your cost by 17 percent?" This type of question allows control for securing a predetermined desired response. Again, the objective is only to gain interest, allowing a natural transition into the proposal.

This technique is most effective in face-to-face selling, but it is also used in mass-market TV commercials:

- Life-insurance commercial: "Who will take care of your family if you're not there?"

- Auto commercial: "When you turn your car on, does it return the favor?"

- Aspirin commercial: "What is the number-one over-the-counter medication used today to prevent heart attacks?"

Whether in face-to-face selling or TV commercials, questions are designed to evoke emotions of joy, optimism, concern, failure, success, or fear—arousing interest and curiosity, thus stimulating the buyer to want to hear more.

If successfully accomplished, a smooth transition into the proposal is achieved.

> *Statement* ~~~~ **DEVELOP STATEMENTS RELATIVE TO THE SELLING OBJECTIVE THAT REQUIRES ADDITIONAL EXPLANATION.**

Statements should be bold in nature, focused on the selling objective, designed to stimulate interest, and in need of additional information to support them. For example:

- "In fifteen minutes, you could save up to 15 percent."

- "Our clients save on average $350 compared to what you are currently spending for the same coverage."

The objective is only to gain interest, engage the buyer, and provide a bridge to the proposal.

> *Exhibit* ~~~~~~~~ **UTILIZE PRODUCT OR SALES AIDS TO AROUSE CURIOSITY AND INTEREST**

The product itself may be used as an exhibit, followed by a statement like, "It produces the best results in five of the six major performance areas required." If the buyer is not familiar with the item, curiosity will be aroused. If the buyer *is* familiar with the product, interest or curiosity is aroused as to why it provided superior performance and in what five areas.

Taking the sales stage by demonstrating the product is one of the most dynamic methods in making your sales points. Buyers in the market for an item that produces results as demonstrated will want more information. Attention is gained, and it's time to move on to the proposal.

> **SENSES ~~~~~~~   APPEAL TO THE BUYER'S SENSES.**

What better way to display product attributes than through the senses? Make use of the buyer's sense of sight, touch, smell, taste, and sound. This approach provides an added dynamic in developing interest.

When possible and advantageous, place the product in the buyer's hands for inspection. Buyers may have reservations about accepting presentation information, but they trust their five senses. Gaining a favorable response via the senses not only provides a gateway to the proposal but also builds product performance acceptance.

THE ONLY OBJECTIVE OF THE OPENING IS TO GAIN INTEREST
AND
PROVIDE A SMOOTH TRANSITION ONTO THE PROPOAL

Landscape Rule #1
Buyers are the gatekeepers, determining the success of a salesperson based on their buying decisions, positive or negative.

Landscape Rule #4

Set yourself apart from the competition.

PROPOSAL

The sole object of the proposal discipline is to gain a positive buying decision. Proposals combine persuasive data, product education, business advantages, and personal benefits to entice the buyer. A good proposal includes an opportunity for conversation, reviewing major considerations by both buyer and seller.

PROPOSAL DISCIPLINES

- **STATE SALES OBJECTIVE**
- **PROVIDE KEY INFORMATION**
- **CONVERT FEATURES TO BENEFITS**
- **PROVIDE PROOF SOURCES**
- **GAIN INFORMATION**

Most buyers (you included) are skeptical or hesitant, having a common mindset known as the FUD Factor when making high-value buying decisions.

FUD Factor: *fear—uncertainty—doubt.*

- Fear of making a bad buying decision.

- Uncertain that the product will perform as presented, or that the company has the ability to deliver in a timely fashion.

- Doubt that the product will provide the benefits as advertised.

PURCHASING DECISIONS ARE BASED ON EVALUATING RISK VERSES VALUE

Individual consumers purchasing personal items like insurance, autos, and televisions exhibit FUD just as corporate buyers do.

Upon transitioning from your opening to the proposal, make an effort to determine buyer mindset, seek out desired benefits, and determine key concerns needing to be addressed.

Generally, buying decisions are based on the Risk to Value Ratio (RVR)—lowest risk to highest value. RVR encompasses all aspects of the proposal, not just the price. Having the lowest price without desired benefits will not win a sale.

Engage the buyer in conversation, avoiding a one-way sales pitch. Develop an open dialogue, establishing effective two-way communications to reduce buyer anxiety. Ask for information, listen, and segregate important issues needing to be addressed from minor issues. Focus the buyer's attention on the purpose of your visit, targeting specific selling objectives.

Communicate key information designed to persuade the buyer, point-by-point, that the product will provide a sufficient level of business and personal benefits to over come the FUD Factor and gain a positive buying decision. Features and benefits must be utilized to satisfy specific areas of importance or buyers concerns, such as product specifications, RVR, product availability, and delivery schedule. Obtaining agreement with benefit statements will assist in gaining the buyer's acceptance of the overall proposal. If the buyer raises an objection or shows doubt and uncertainty, the seller must be prepared to respond in a way that regains the buyer's confidence and agreement. Sales proposals rely heavily on effective communication, with well-chosen words and phrases, sources of proof, charts, graphs, and demonstrations, all of which must support the seller's claims.

During the proposal, product knowledge and preparation come together. Individually tailored presentation materials, charts, graphs, in-house corporate sales literature, and proof sources should be at the ready. You may not need all your material; that will depend on individual buyer requirements and sought-after features and benefits. However, the material must be available if needed.

Being prepared to satisfy the buyer's expectation for acquiring significant information is a component of the sales process that cannot be underestimated or overlooked. Nothing kills a sale faster than failing to provide critical decision-making information. The better prepared you are, the greater confidence and self-assurance you'll show when taking the sales stage.

THE PROPOSAL OBJECTIVE IS TO GAIN A POSITIVE BUYING DECISION

Landscape Rule # 3
Sales success comes from the 80 percent that will buy if sold—the Rule of 80.

Landscape Rule # 4
Set yourself apart from the competition.

Landscape Rule # 5
Establish sales-call objectives.

Landscape Rule # 7
Mental Toolbox

FEATURES & BENEFITS

Features Tell ~~ Benefits Sell

FEATURES

> **FEATURES ARE THE INHERENT CHARACTERISTICS THAT DISTINGUISH WHAT A PRODUCT OFFERS. THEY ARE TANGIBLE AND CAN BE PERCEIVED BY THE SENSES.**

A product generally possesses multiple features. Cars, for example, offer features like power steering, air-conditioning, antilock brakes, CD player, cruise control, power widows, and GPS. These features are common, but what about products or services like electronics, insurance policies, or family trusts where features are not common and perhaps not readily known? Features must be communicated before the buyer can understand what your product offers.

FEATURES DEFINE WHAT A PRODUCT OFFERS

BENEFITS

> BENEFITS ANSWER THE QUESTION—WHAT DOES A FEATURE DO FOR ME? BENEFITS MAY BE TANGIBLE OR INTANGIBLE AND MAY NOT BE READILY APPARENT. A SINGLE FEATURE MAY PROVIDE SEVERAL BENEFITS.

BENEFITS STATE THE VALUE FEATURES PROVIDE

A complete understanding of all product features and benefits is essential, as these represent core attributes that a buyer will use to make a purchasing decision. Buyers purchase a product not for what it is, but what it can do for their business or for them personally. Features offer information about the product, while benefits transfer product information into perceived value.

Not all features or benefits are of equal importance to all buyers. Salespeople must query the buyer for insight into his or her individual purchasing requirements—outlining product features, determining high-value benefits coinciding with those features, and focusing on those benefits.

Does cruise control provide the same benefit for a person who drives only in New York City as it does for a salesperson traveling the entire state of Texas? Air-conditioning is a must-have in Arizona, but would it be considered a major benefit in Alaska? Presenting all the features and benefits of a product to the buyer and seeing what sticks—the "spaghetti approach"—is ineffective, wastes time, and at worst costs buyer interest and attention. The key to making a sale is zeroing in and providing the buyer with sought-after, high-value benefits.

Individuals requiring specific product benefits will not considered purchasing if the desired "make or break" benefits are not provided, regardless of other features and benefits offered.

Needing a new television for the bedroom recently, I asked my sons to pick one up for me. Since I wasn't particular, as it was just for the bedroom, there were several features that were negotiable, such as size, wall mount or tabletop, and brand name. However, I required two make-or-break benefits that were nonnegotiable: the new TV had to have a remote (for ease of on-of and changing channels) and a sleep timer (automatic off at selected time). Regardless of all other benefits provided, if these two were not included, I wasn't interested.

A simple way to determine what a buyer considers important is to ask one simple question: "What are the major factors you consider in making a buying decision?" By answering the question, the buyer reveals the major benefits required and provides specific direction for guiding the sales conversation toward an affirmative buying decision. Not all buyers place the same value or importance on the same feature.

As a young salesperson, I was given my first major sales opportunity with responsibility to sell a new product to a leading retail chain. It felt as though my entire future and career rested on this one sale. I memorized all the sales information provided by the company. Filled with product knowledge, selling confidence high, I was certain that all sales information must be supplied to insure sales success. Nothing would be left to chance, I would start at page one of the thirty-page sales brochure and make sure that all information was delivered.

The buyer, an older gentleman, sat quietly and listened respectively as I rattled on, endlessly talking and turning brochure pages. Upon concluding the final page, I asked if he was ready to purchase. He quickly responded, "Too much information! I am confused and not sure at this time." It was clear the *no sale* sign was up that day, and I could not understand why.

I then asked one simple question: "What are the major factors you consider in making a new product purchase decision?" The buyer expressed specific sought-after business benefits and those of personal importance. A subsequent appointment was established. Armed with specific buying requirements, I focused my presentation only on the features and benefits indicated as make-or-break, avoiding issues of little conscience. The sale was gained.

THE MISSION OF A SALESPERSON IS NOT TO BE INFORMATIVE BUT TO BE PERSUASIVE AND MAKE A SALE

CONVERTING FEATURES INTO BENEFITS

Merely pointing out the features of a product is not enough. If features are not converted to benefits, the most persuasive part of the selling message has not been delivered. Benefits may not always be readily apparent; assuming buyers naturally understand and appreciate them is risky and can be a costly mistake. Benefits or value must be conveyed to the buyer for each meaningful feature provided. This is known as converting features into benefits.

Feature Statement	*Benefit Conversion Statement*	*Benefit Statement*
Convey product feature	"Which means . . ." "The benefit to you is . . ." "What this does for you is . . ." "The advantage this provides is . . ."	Provide a meaningful benefit to the buyer

Remember, buying decisions are based on benefits—what it does for the buyer—not on features. The greater number of features converted into meaningful benefits, the greater opportunity for the buying gate to open.

Even a simple item like a yellow plastic pencil provides several meaningful benefits. Benefit conversion statements provide the bridge from feature to benefit

Feature: Adjustable lead.
Benefit conversion statement:
   "The advantage this provides is
   - —always having a sharp writing point."
   - —does not require sharpening like wood pencils."

> "The benefit to you is
> - —lead can be retracted to insure clothing is not marked."

Feature: #2 Lead
Benefit conversion statement:
> "Which means
> - —strong material for writing, not prone to breaking."

Feature: Pocket clasp
Benefit conversion statement:
> "The benefit to you is
> - —pencil won't fall out of shirt pocket."

Feature: Eraser
Benefit conversion statement:
> "What this does for you is
> - —gives you an easy way to edit or correct mistakes without leaving documents in a scratched-out mess."

Feature: Light and fits the hand
Benefit conversion statement:
> "The advantage this provides is
> - —comfortable and easy to use."

The more meaningful benefits provided, the easier it will be for the buyer to make the purchase. Many salespeople make an enormous mistake in only telling product features and not supplying product benefits.

FEATURES TELL ~~ BENEFITS SELL

Landscape Rule # 3

Sales success comes from the eighty percent that will buy if SOLD. "Rule of 80"

Landscape Rule # 4

Set yourself apart from the competition.

PROOF SOURCE

A *proof source* is physical evidence that supports a selling statement. Proof sources used in the proper context—supporting specific proposal claims—overcome buyers' FUD or objection. This allows the seller to gain agreement and build the buyer's confidence in the product being proposed. Not every selling statement requires a proof source; in fact, proof sources should be limited to supporting critical information, key features and benefits, or overcoming an objection.

A proof source is only effective if it pertains to the subject being discussed or questioned. Stay on point. Remember, the spaghetti approach is ineffective, waste time, and loses buyer interest and attention. Less is more. Only use proof sources when and where needed to gain or regain buyers' confidence and agreement.

PROOF SOURCES

- **Independent Third-Party Reports**
- **Graphs, Charts, and Diagrams**
- **Product Demonstrations**
- **Customer Testimonials**

Most buyers readily accept the validity of third-party information as a proof source and allow it to assist them in their buying decisions. Unsolicited, independent, third-party reports excluding sellers' prejudice—such as trade journals, industry reports, newspaper articles, and documents—provide unbiased observations and opinions. Favorable reports that support the selling message increase buyer acceptance and reduce FUD, making it easier for the buyer to say yes to the proposal.

Graphs, Charts, and Diagrams: Illustrations based on third-party information provide effective proof sources for easy visual comprehension and quick information reference. Use graphs and charts to dramatize a point, compare sales trends, and forecast future conditions. There is only one rule regarding the number of graphs and charts contained in a proposal: don't overdo it.

Demonstrate the product, point out the features and convert them to meaningful benefits. If the product is easy to use, get the buyer involved (use the senses) in trying it out, following the salesperson's instructions.

Contracts are proof source for agreements entered into and can be used as a strong selling tool. In many cases, contracts are the center-piece of a presentation.

Customer Testimonials: When completing a sale and having gained buyer satisfaction, ask for a personal testimonial that can be shared with other clients. Testimonies from individuals or businesses are highly regarded by individual consumers and by buyers within a comparable industry or business community.

LANDSCAPE RULE # 4
Set yourself apart from the competition.

BUYING SIGNALS

Buying signals indicate a high level of interest and suggests a possible willingness to buy. They can surface at any time during the presentation. Listen for questions indicating high interest in specific feature or benefit areas, or in evaluating current status versus proposed change. Watch for positive body language.

Listen for these *questions* from the buyer:

- What is the price?

- When will it be available?

- Have my competitors already purchased this product?

- What is the minimum purchase requirement?

- Will there be promotional support?

These are good indicators that the buyer is interested in what you're selling. Make sure you can quickly respond with an answer that clinches the sale.

Statements and behaviors along these lines indicate that the buyer *evaluating* your product or service in a positive manner:

- Likes benefits of product being presented versus current product offering

- Prefers proposed cost to current cost

- Perceives proposed product to be of higher quality than current product

- Continues to re-examine sample product

- Rereads proposal literature

Support the buyer in these impressions and evaluations to further the likelihood of a sale.

Buyer often display nonverbal *body language* like:

- Attentiveness and interest in proposal

- Nodding of head in a positive manner and gestures that indicate agreement with presented material

- Body shifts from a tense and guarded posture to a more relaxed open posture

When receiving buying signals during the proposal, carefully consider the buyer's reception to the presentation and his or her personality, and then select the appropriate closing technique "tool" to seal the deal and tap into the Rule of 80.

LANDSCAPE RULE # 7
Mental Toolbox

CLOSE

Closing is the final discipline, and it calls for action. Never miss an opportunity to ask a buyer to buy. A professional buyer or individual client expects you to ask. If you don't, you only shortchange yourself.

The close is not an amazing magical act—it is a selling discipline, and the action step in the selling process. Closing is the next logical and natural step following an effective proposal that provides business and personal benefits and overcomes objections.

The secret to closing is recognizing when to close and selecting the appropriate techniques. Never back a buyer into a decision-making corner using closed-ended questions requiring a yes or no response—those are appropriate for your opening, but not for your closing. Think of the last time a salesperson put you in a buying-decision corner. Your reaction more than likely was negative, and it may have cost the salesperson a sale. Open-ended questions requiring a narrative response lead to additional conversation, giving you feedback from the buyer. If an objection arises, it can be addressed at this time.

Professional tradespeople know that using the appropriate tool for a task makes it easier to accomplish the job. If a Philips-head screwdriver is required, a flathead won't get the job done. An auto-mechanic's toolbox may stand as high as five feet just to contain the required amount of tools necessary to complete specific tasks.

Closing techniques are selling tools designed to assist in finalizing the sale and, if necessary, overcoming objections. The proper tools must be utilized to attain success with the 80 percent that will buy if sold.

Nationally, millions of dollars in business goes unrealized because of a lack of action supporting a positive buying decision.

Closing requires more than merely receiving a positive buying decision from the buyer. The job isn't done until the paper work is completed. Securing a signed order or contract, efficiently processed including all administrative requirements, is an important step that can't be neglected. The sales cycle is complete when the seller fulfills the terms of the agreement and the buyer renders payment.

LANDSCAPE RULE # 1
Buyers are the gatekeepers determining the success of a salesperson based on their buying decisions, positive or negative.

LANDSCAPE RULE # 7
Mental Toolbox

CLOSING TECHNIQUES

RIGHT TOOL FOR THE JOB

- ASK FOR THE ORDER
- CHOICE
- SUMMARY
- URGENCY
- TRIAL
- ASSUMPTIVE

Closing techniques are among the most important tools sellers can have in their toolbox. Buyer personalities and a changing business climate require skillful deployment of various closing techniques. Successful salespeople have high closing rates because their toolbox has been developed with closing techniques ready to use based on any given circumstance. Prior to exiting the proposal and entering the "close," these sellers select a closing technique aligned with the buyer's mental position. Closing techniques may be use individually or in combination.

Make it easy for the buyer to say yes and open the buying gate. Use the right tool.

ASK FOR THE ORDER

ASK FOR THE ORDER ~~~~~~~~~~	**ASK THE BUYER TO PURCHASE**
EXAMPLE ~~~~~~~~	**"WE COVERED ALL THE ISSUES, HOW ABOUT WE WRITE THE ORDER UP?"**

BUYERS EXPECT YOU TO ASK THEM TO BUY

Asking for the order is the most direct and straight forward closing technique. How better to obtain an order than simply asking for it? Buyers expect you to ask them to buy.

Asking a client to buy does not require a high level of selling skill. However, many salespeople are afraid of rejection or that an objection may arise that they are unable to field. More lost sales are due to not asking for the order—poor closing skills—than any other reason.

When asking for the order, make you question direct, with well-chosen words or phrases that make it clear you're requesting action. Be careful, though, not to back the buyer into a decision—making corner.

Consider the effort expended in gaining an appointment, developing presentation materials, connecting, opening, and delivering an effective proposal. All of that will all add up to nothing if you don't at least ask for the order. You only cheat yourself if you don't ask.

IF YOU DON'T ASK, YOU DON'T GET—YOU LOOSE!

If an objection is raised when closing, the next step is to determine what the objection is, resolve it to both parties' satisfaction, and close again.

CHOICE CLOSE

CHOICE CLOSE ~~~~~	**PROVIDES A CHOICE BETWEEN TWO ALTERNATIVE BUYING ACTIONS, BOTH OF WHICH ARE FAVORABLE TO THE SELLER.**
EXAMPLE ~~~~~~~~~~	"WOULD YOU LIKE DELIVERY ON THE FIRST OR THE FIFTEENTH?"
	"WILL YOU NEED FIVE OR EIGHT CASES TO COVER ADDITIONAL SALES DURING THIS PROMOTION?"
	"WOULD YOU LIKE THE POLICY TO BE IN EFFECT FOR TWELVE OR TWENTY-FOUR MONTHS?"

The choice close is simple and direct. Put forward a question offering a choice of action, with the result of either choice satisfying the selling objective. By offering a choice, you shift the buyer's thought process from a "yes or no" buying decision to the choices presented. The buyer's focus shifts to selecting the best purchasing alternative of the choices provided.

When you ask a choice question like "Would you prefer vanilla or chocolate?" the buyer focuses on selecting the most desirable flavor—a decision that assumes ice cream will be purchased.

If an objection is raised when closing, the next step is to determine what the objection is, resolve it to both parties' satisfaction, and close again.

SUMMARY CLOSE

> **SUMMARY CLOSE ~~ RECAPS BUYER'S ACCEPTANCE OF HIGH—VALUE BENEFITS PROVIDED IN THE PROPOSAL. AN EXCELLENT WAY TO ACHIEVE THE "YES" MODE IN GAINING A POSITIVE DECISION.**

The summary close works best when buyers have demonstrated positive interest or acceptance of major business or personal benefits provided within the proposal. Summarizing and recapping each major benefit reduces FUD, provides positive reinforcement, and strengthens agreement when closing. When making your summary, utilize reinforcement phrases:

- "You liked _____" (restate the benefit)
- "We agreed _____ provided . . ." (restate agreed upon value)
- "You stated _____ would . . ." (restate value)

Avoid areas where positive levels of interest or acceptance were not demonstrated.

Imagine a bobble-head doll on the dashboard of your car with its head moving up and down in a yes motion. It is almost impossible to go directly to a side-to-side negative motion. Mentally, buyers will convince themselves. Summarize and gain buyer agreement with multiple high-value benefits supporting a positive buying decision. The greater number of benefits agreed with, the easier it is for buyers to say yes and more difficult it is to say no to your closing. Open the buying gate. Get the buyer's heads moving up and down.

If an objection is raised when closing, the next step is to determine what the objection is, resolve it to both parties' satisfaction, and close again.

URGENCY CLOSE

Use the urgency technique when there are special offers of limited quantity—such as special pricing or payment terms—or when time is of the essence and immediate action is required. Buyers are motivated to participate in special buying opportunities that provide extra value and benefits.

URGENCY CLOSE ~~~	USED TO GIVE THE BUYER A REASON TO MAKE A POSITIVE BUYING DECISION AND TAKE IMMEDIATE ACTION.
EXAMPLE ~~~~~~~~~~	"PROMOTION ENDS ON FRIDAY WE NEED TO PLACE AN ORDER NOW TO TAKE ADVANTAGE OF THIS SPECIAL PRICE."
	"WAREHOUSE INVENTORIES ARE LOW. TO MAINTAIN INVENTORY LEVELS TO MEET SALES DEMAND, AN ORDER NEDDS TO BE PLACED NOW."
	"YOUR PREMIUM WILL INCREASE BY 17 PERCENT IF YOU WAIT TO YOUR NEXT BIRTHDAY. NOW IS THE TIME TO SIGN UP TO KEEP THE SAME LOW PREMIUM FOR THE NEXT PERIOD."

Promotions and special offers provide extra value to clients and further develop business relationships and sales. Offering special buying opportunities and conditions of sale—time sensitive, limited quantity, price reduction—develop a positive relationship, and buyers feel that the sales agent has their best interest at heart. All specials need to be presented; it's not the salesperson's job to decide which the customer wants. It is important that all clients are presented equally. Nothing disturbs clients more than finding out they did not receive the same buying opportunity as others, even if they would have chosen not to participate.

Urgency closes are not confined to special offers or promotions. Businesses do not want to be out of stock—out of stock means out of business. Low inventory and fear of potential lost sales provide the perfect opportunity to use the urgency close.

If an objection is raised when closing, the next step is to determine what the objection is, resolve it to both parties' satisfaction, and close again.

TRIAL CLOSE

Positive acceptance of product information prior to the conclusion of a proposal provides the opportunity for a trial close. Watch for those buying signals.

> *Trial Close* ~~~~~ **QUESTIONS ASKED AT VARIOUS TIMES DURING THE SALES CONVERSATION TO DETERMINE IF THE BUYER IS READY TO CLOSE. A TRIAL CLOSE <u>ASKS FOR AN OPINION NOT A DECISION</u>.**
>
> *Example* ~~~~~~~ **"HOW DOES THIS OFFER FIT WITH YOUR GOALS?"**
>
> **"WOULD THE BENEFITS OUTLINED SO FAR MAKE YOUR BUSINESS RUN SMOOTHER AND MAKE YOUR LIFE EASIER?"**
>
> **"DO YOU FEEL THAT THIS PROVIDES ADEQUATE COVERAGE?"**

The trial close gives the seller an opportunity to determine if the time is right to close without disrupting the flow of the presentation. Trial closes may be used anytime during the sales presentation to determine interest and see how close the buyer is to making a decision.

A trial close asks the buyer for an opinion rather than a decision. This provides an opportunity to evaluate the buyer's mental position regarding the information supplied during the presentation. Open-ended questions are best when using the trial close, as they provide greater feedback and understanding of the buyer's mental position. If a strong positive response is given, select an additional closing technique and gain the order.

Car salespeople use this technique throughout their sales encounter with a potential buyer. In fact, they may open with a trial close:

- "Is this the car you want to drive home today?"

- "That is a great choice. Is that the color you want?"

- "How would you like to drive it home today for as little as $299 a month?"

Top salespeople say "Close early and often". The trial close allows the seller to make several subtle closing attempts without offending the buyer.

If an objection is raised when closing, the next step is to determine what the objection is, resolve it to both parties' satisfaction, and close again.

ASSUMPTIVE CLOSE

With the assumptive technique, the seller assumes the buyer is willing to purchase based on positive reaction to the majority of product features and benefits.

> *Assumptive Close ~* **SALESPERSON PROJECTS COMPLETE CONFIDENCE A POSITIVE BUYING DECISION HAS BEEN MADE. SALESPERSON ASKS A LEADING QUESTION OR MAKES A STATEMENT CALLING FOR ACTION.**
>
> *Example ~~~~~~~* **"SIGN HERE TO RECEIVE ALL THE BENEFITS WE DISCUSSED."**

The salesperson places a contract in front of the buyer and provides a pen for his or her signature. This challenges the buyer to act.

When selling products requiring shipping and delivery, take out an order form and start filling in required information. Request a purchase-order number and quaintness to be ordered.

Ask specific questions required for filling in contract information on intangibles like personal services and insurance. Buyers will provide information and proceed with the buying process or indicate they are not quite ready to commit. An assumptive closing will gain a sale or unearth questions or objections that may need to be addressed.

If an objection is raised when closing, the next step is to determine what the objection is, resolve it to both parties' satisfaction, and close again.

LANDSCAPE RULE # 1
Buyers are the gatekeepers, determining the success of a salesperson based on their buying decisions, positive or negative.

LANDSCAPE RULE # 7
Mental Toolbox

WHEN MINDS DON'T MEET

HANDLING OBJECTION SKILLS SEPARATES THE SALESPERSON FROM THE ORDER TAKER, AND THE PRESENTER FROM THE CLOSER

OBJECTIONS

Selling starts when the buyer raises an objection or says no. Until then, it's just a presentation. A significant improvement in closing sales can be attained through the effective handling of objections. Don't confuse questions (seeking additional information), with objections (resistance).

DEFINITION OF OBJECTION

> **AN OBJECTION IS BUYER RESISTANCE, A BARRIER STANDING IN THE WAY OF AN AFFIRMATIVE RESPONSE TO THE SALES PROPOSAL.**

Providing a rebuttal to an objection with the same information already provided over and over expecting a different result is sales insanity. I personally witnessed this while working for a Fortune 500 company that required sales personnel to gain targeted levels of distribution when introducing new products. If a salesperson was initially unsuccessful in gaining new product distribution with a high-value account, the sales manager would accompany him or her on a second sales call and present the same material as previously delivered. When they were unsuccessful, the manager would be accompanied by the next level of management, who again presented the same material, and so on up the chain of command. Presenting the same material over and over expecting a different result isn't persistence—it's insanity.

Avoid sales insanity. Identify the areas of major resistance and provide a solution that is satisfactory to both buyer and seller. The fact is that buyers will raise objections for a variety of reasons. Skill in handling and resolving objections directly enhances close rates. Break the barriers of resistance and tap into the 80 percent who will buy if sold.

Landscape Rule # 1
Buyers are the gatekeepers determining the success of a salesperson based on their buying decisions, positive or negative.

Landscape Rule # 3
Sales success comes from the eighty percent that will buy if SOLD. Rule of 80.

Landscape Rule # 7
Mental Toolbox

PERSONAL ATTITUDE TOWARDES OBJECTIONS

A fishing equipment company sent salespeople to an isolated island to generate new business. After a week, the sales manager received an e-mail from one of the salespeople: "Returning back to the mainland, as it is impossible to sell fishing equipment. No one here eats fish." Within a few minutes, the sales manager received a second e-mail, from another salesperson: "Enclosed find orders for 250 rods and reels and other assorted items. Opportunity unrestricted. No one here knows how to fish."

Anticipate initial buyer resistance when cold-calling or visiting a client the first time. Expect buyers to voice objections if they have areas of concern. Buyers will want to know:

- "Who are you?"

- "Why are you calling on me?"

- "Is what you have to say important?"

- "How will I benefit?"

How do you mentally view objections? Do you experience the FUD Factor when receiving objections? Respond to the following statements to determine your personal mindset regarding objections.

1. Objection-handling skill coincides with a salesperson's personal attitude towards objections.

   ☐ Agree
   ☐ Disagree

2. A buyer's objections indicate that there is no interest in my sales proposal.

   ☐ Agree
   ☐ Disagree

3. An objection may show a buyer's concern about the validity of my proposal.

   ☐ Agree
   ☐ Disagree

4. Buyers' objections signal a need for more information.

   ☐ Agree
   ☐ Disagree

5. Strong opposition to objections usually leads to making a sale.

   ☐ Agree
   ☐ Disagree

6. Buyers are sometimes reluctant to bring their true objections into the open.

   ☐ Agree
   ☐ Disagree

7. Objections may indicate a lack of understanding by the buyer.

☐ Agree
☐ Disagree

Objections are negotiable differences between buyer and seller that must be resolved to the satisfaction of both parties to move the buying process forward. It is imperative to have a clear understanding of the objection and provide an acceptable solution. Handling objections in a timely and efficient manner assists in securing the sale and eliminating competitive intrusion. Open-mindedness, a positive attitude, and personal confidence are required.

The following responses to the statements above indicate that you're in the right frame of mind. If you had different answers, you'll need to change your attitude.

1. **Agree**—Positive attitudes produce positive alternatives while negative attitudes accept defeat.

2. **Disagree**—Objections indicate buyer interest. An objection would not be raised if there wasn't interest.

3. **Agree**—Buyers need to be convinced. Supporting evidence and proof sources must be used to overcome specific objections.

4. **Agree**—Objections in many cases are just questions looking for additional information.

5. **Disagree**—An appropriate response is called for, not opposition. Strong opposition leads to conflict, cementing buyers' resistance.

6. **Agree**—Buyers sometime offer false objections. Determining the hidden, real objection is something you must accomplish to make a sale.

7. **Agree**—Poorly presented information or complicated material may cause buyers misunderstanding or confusion.

ATTITUDE TOWARD OBJECTIONS

Objections are a fundamental part of the sales process. Once you've accepted the idea that objections are to be expected and are a normal part of the sales process, a much sounder philosophical attitude can be developed in which to approach them.

OBJECTIONS ARE WINDOWS TO BUYERS RESISTANCE

They are windows through which the seller can see what that buyer considers important that was not covered satisfactorily in the proposal. Additionally, the seller gains invaluable information on how close or how far apart the buyer and seller are and what is required to achieve a sale.

WHEN HANDLING OBJECTIONS AVOID MAKING ENEMIES

Regardless of the level of contradiction or how intense the disagreement or buyer's persistence in trying to argue, *do not argue with the buyer.*

Arguing increases buyers' resistance and makes it personal. This will only lead to losing a sales and perhaps a customer.

NEW OBJECTIONS?

The same few reoccurring objections represent 80 to 90 percent of total objections encountered. These should be anticipated, planned for, and solutions incorporated in the proposal. A new objection may occur, but if you use the right tools, the buying gate can still be unlocked.

NEVER MAGNIFY AN OBJECTION

Not all objections carry the same level of importance. Generally, only one or two make-or-break objections may occur. However, the majority of objections are minor and may not have a major impact in a buying decision. Objections should never be exaggerated or expanded beyond the buyers' level of concern.

Don't build a mountain out of a mole hill.

HIDDEN OBJECTIONS

At times, buyers present objections to disguise or hide the real reasons for their unwillingness to purchase. Ask questions, identify the actual objection, and provide a solution.

WHY BUYERS PRESENT OBJECTIONS

NEED FOR ADDITIONAL INFORMATION
The buyer may feel uncomfortable with the current level of information regarding the products or programs.

MISUNDERSTANDING INFORMATION
Objections occur when sales-proposal material is misunderstood or the buyer only partially understanding it.

NOT CONVINCED OF THE VALUE
Most objections are based on buyer's perception that the investment outweighs the benefits or value received

SOLVE MY "PROBLEM"
Buyers present objections when faced with in-house issues that need to be resolved, but a solution has not been initiated. The seller must identify the problem and provide a solution.

HANDLING OBJECTIONS CHECK LIST

Check these items off as you present your proposal to make sure you address buyers' potential objections.

- ☐ Anticipate all common objections that may arise and include responses in the sales proposal. Have additional support material ready, including proof sources, for use if and when required. Honor the Boy Scout motto: "Be prepared."

- ☐ During the sales conversation, listen carefully and identify buyer objections. It is paramount to identify and separate minor objection from major make-or-break objections. Avoid turning minor objections into large ones. Remember, don't make a mountain out of a mole hill.

- ☐ View objections as windows of opportunity in determining what a buyer considers important in making a buying decision.

- ☐ Have a positive attitude. Answer objections as if they were simple questions, utilizing the appropriate technique.

- ☐ After a sales encounter, self-critique your performance. Determine your skill and comfort level in handling objections.

Analyze how well you handled the objections and what techniques you used. Make a note or a list of objections you found difficult to answer and develop answers for future use.

Landscape Rule #1
Buyers are the gatekeepers, determining the success of a salesperson based on their buying decisions, positive or negative.

Landscape Rule #3
Sales success comes from the 80 percent who will buy if sold—the Rule of 80.

Landscape Rule #7
Use your mental toolbox.

HANDLING OBJECTION TECHNIQUES

A significant close rate can be attained through effective implementation of handling objection techniques.

TECHNIQUES
- **DELAY**
- **YES, HOWEVER**
- **EXONERATE BUYER FROM BLAME**
- **DENIAL**
- **TURN OBJECTION INTO A**
- **POSITIVE SOLVE THE PROBLEM**

DELAY

The delay technique is effective by postponing rebuttal to an objection. Objections must be resolved to the satisfaction of the buyer, however not necessarily needing to be answered when raised.

SALES SITUATION

1. A minor objection is raised, to which rebuttal information is addressed later in the proposal material.

2. Salesperson does not have an answer for an objection when raised and requires time to develop one.

3. ### HANDLING OBJECTION TECHNIQUE

DELAY

Example:
1. "That's a good question. I believe it will be covered later in the proposal."

2. "Hold on to that thought. We will get to it."

RESULT

1. Allows an objection to be address at the appropriate time, as an answer is provided in the proposal material. Seller maintains control by keeping the sales conversation on track.

2. If an objection rebuttal is not top of mind, allows time for seller to develop a response. This also acts as a gage in determining the importance of an objection. If the objection is minor, it will not resurface. If the objection is major, it will be restated, providing insight to its level of importance to the buyer.

The biggest mistake a salesperson can make when an objection is raised is to respond, "I don't know, but I will get an answer for you." The *no sale* sign just went up, and the buyer expects at a later date a follow-up response to what may have only been a minor concern or question. Instead, use the delaying technique when you don't have a ready reply for an objection. If the objection is minor, it may not be raised again. If it is important, it will resurface.

If an objection reoccurs at the conclusion of the proposal, and you are unable to formulate an acceptable response, obtain a complete understanding of the objection. Now is the time to respond, "I don't know, but I will get an answer for you." Follow up by asking, "Is this the only issue keeping you from buying?" This will provide a gauge in determining how close or how far you are from closing the sale. If the buyer says yes, gain buyer commitment by asking, "If I can satisfy your concern on this issue, do we have a deal?"

If there are other issues to be addressed, they will surface at this time. If not, the seller knows what must be provided to close the sale. Schedule an appointment for a follow-up presentation.

YES, HOWEVER

SALES SITUATION

- Seller agrees with a portion of the buyer's objection, but disagrees with the overall position the buyer expressed.

HANDLING OBJECTION TECHNIQUE

YES, HOWEVER

Example:

- "Yes, I appreciate your concern, however (. . .)" (give your rebuttal and justify your position)

RESULT

- Your initial "yes" indicates agreement and aids in lowering buyer resistance, establishes some common ground. "However" suggests additional consideration should be given to the seller's position.

This technique is familiar to us from childhood as "yes, but." When using it in a sales situation, though, it's better to use "yes, however," which invites discussion, rather than "yes, but," which signals disagreement and a desire to change the buyer's position.

In many cases, objections occur because of limited information or an incomplete realization of the benefits provided. The buyer needs additional explanation. The "yes, however" technique allows for agreement with what the buyer understands and the seller agrees with, reduces resistance, establishes common ground, and provides a bridge for additional conversation addressing areas of misunderstanding or disagreement.

When positions differ, avoid confrontation, stick to the facts, furnish supporting proof sources, and provide a positive resolution to the objection. Do not argue or make it personal.

EXONERATE BUYER FROM BLAME

SALES SITUATION

- Buyer raises an objection based on misunderstanding of information provided during the sales proposal.

HANDLING OBJECTION TECHNIQUE

EXONERATE BUYER FROM BLAME

Example:

- "I'm sorry I did not cover that as completely as I should have. Please allow me to clarify . . . ."

- "I'm sorry if I misled you into thinking . . . ."

- "I apologize for not being as clear as I should have been. Please allow me to clarify . . . ."

RESULT

- Seller takes responsible for misunderstanding, allowing buyer to save face, maintain ego, and receive clarification of information.

Complex material may intimidate a buyer and lead to confusion or misunderstanding of information. In some cases, buyers may become defensive about their inability to grasp the information. Exonerating the buyer from blame allows the seller to re-explain complex material in a manner that increases understanding.

If a presentation is delivered in a disorganized manner, misunderstanding can occur. Don't place the blame on the buyer for a poor presentation. If an objection is raised because of confusion or misinterpretation, exonerate the buyer and accept responsibly for the confusion. This will allow the buyer to receive information in the specific areas in question with an open mind. Never speak down in a condescending manner, causing the buyer to feel inferior.

DENIAL

SALES SITUATION

- Buyer raises an objection based on rumors or false or inaccurate information.

HANDLING OBJECTION TECHNIQUE

DENIAL

Example:
- "I'm sorry, but that information is incorrect. The fact of the matter is . . . ."

RESULT

- Over comes objection by providing accurate information, dispelling previous beliefs based on misunderstood, false, or misleading information.

Sellers must take a strong position when confronted with inaccurate information, misinformation, or negative rumors fostered by a competitor or the media. The adverse impact on the buyer must be dispelled quickly. Without hesitation, provide accurate information using third-party proof sources, product demonstration, customer testimonials, and personal reassurance reinforcing the facts.

This technique requires a firm stance based on facts and may lead to some initial disagreement by the buyer. The seller must be prepared to dispute inaccurate information or erroneous accusations without arguing or making it personal. The truth is always the seller's best weapon, and if presented properly it will win the day.

Until unwarranted beliefs are discredited, it is more than likely the *no sale* sign will remain up.

ASK QUESTIONS

SALES SITUATION   • Seller needs a greater understanding of a specific objection or why the buyer is saying no.
HANDLING OBJECTION TECHNIQUE   ***ASK QUESTIONS***   Example: • "What if I could eliminate your concern of (objection)?"   • "What is your major objection to buying today?"   • "Why not purchase now?"
RESULT   • Gaining insight to the buyer's hesitation and clear understanding of the objection allows the seller to develop a solution.

This objection—handling technique is straightforward and is one of the most effective ways to determine where the bottleneck lies in closing the sale.

Asking open-ended, probing question stimulates conversation and allows you to understand the buyer's actual concerns. A series of questions may be required to actually determine the extent and depth of the resistance.

Listening skills are extremely important, and you must exercise them to their fullest to accurately understand what the buyer is objecting to. When all else fails, the final question to be asked is, "What will it take to do business with you?"

There is no room for misunderstanding an objection. Providing a response to an objection based on misunderstanding will not offer a satisfactory resolution to the buyer. To ensure complete understanding, summarize the objection and restate ("My understanding of your concern is . . . ."). If misunderstanding prevails, ask the buyer to clarify the objection.

TURN OBJECTION INTO A POSITIVE

SALES SITUATION

- Buyer raises an objection which parallels a major benefit contained within the proposal.

HANDLING OBJECTION TECHNIQUE

TURN OBJECTION INTO A POSITIVE
Example:
- "I'm glad you voiced your concern. I think that this issue is solved by (cite proposal benefit)."

RESULT

- Capitalizes on product benefit, overcoming objection.

Glass half full or half empty? Supply an opposing viewpoint demonstrating how the product benefit outweighs the minimal negative being raised. Providing positive product value dissipates the perceived drawback.

Many times, the answer to an objection lies within the product itself. Objections may be raised because of a lack of understanding of what the product does or how it works. This generally occurs with highly technical products and can be overcome by demonstration and education. This handling objection technique turns lemons into lemonade.

SOLVE THE PROBLEM

SALES SITUATION

- An objection is raised, but it is one based on internal problems unrelated to the product or proposal.

- For example, "I would like to add your product, but the shipping carrier you mentioned only delivers us on Friday, and our warehouse does not accept Friday deliveries."

HANDLING OBJECTION TECHNIQUE

SOLVE THE PROBLEM
Example:
- "No problem. We'll use a different carrier. What day would be best for you to take delivery?"

RESULT

- Solves the problem by meeting the warehouse delivery requirement.

Flexibility and working together with individuals and companies are the cornerstones for solving mutual business problems.

Introducing a new product, I proudly placed the item on the buyer's desk. Without any conversation, the buyer responded, "Not interested."

I had but one reply: "Why?"

The buyer informed me he had an item in the warehouse that was not selling, and at the current rate of sale, it would be at least five months before any new item could be considered.

I asked for and received his cost value of the "dead" inventory in the warehouse. With introductory and promotional allowances, I quickly calculated the quantity of product I'd have to sell to allow me to buy out the "dead" inventory.

I suggested that the buyer could sell his current inventory to me at his cost value and replace it with my new item as a solution to his problem.

The deal was struck, and the buyer was happy to offload the "dead" inventory. I gained new distribution within authorized spending limits and enjoyed five months of sales and profits that would not otherwise have been realized. A win for both parties.

Not all problems can be solved, but always investigate the issues at hand. Explore all avenues and consider all valid solutions.

COMMITMENT

IT'S YOUR CAREER—

YOU'RE EARNING POWER—

YOU'RE RESPONSIBILTY-

YOUR DECISION

Life is nothing but a series of decisions. The decisions made today impact the quality of life you'll enjoy or have to endure in the future.

Positive decisions produce positive results. Procrastination encourages not making a decision, resulting in no change.

NO DECISION BECOMES THE DECISION

On a hot summer day, three frogs were sitting on a log. Two decided to jump into the water. How many frogs are left on the log—one, two or three?

Three frogs are still sitting on the log, as no action was taken by any of the frogs. A decision made without positive supporting action becomes nothing more than wishful thinking, ensuring that next week, next month, and next year will only repeat today's status quo.

Changing technology produces a more sophisticated buyer. Individuals who refuse to develop or improve personal selling skills will not fully reap the rewards of a sales career. The first step to success is making a decision to improve personal skill levels. The key ingredients are desire, dedication, developing a plan for improvement, and taking action.

PERSONAL SKILL DEVELOPMENT:

To start on your plan for improvement, determine your areas of strength and the areas you need to work on.

1. Identify areas where improvement is needed.

    ☐ Connecting: Are you just another sales person?

    ☐ Opening: Are you gaining interest and involvement?

    ☐ Proposal: Are you providing value and gaining buyer conviction?

    ☐ Closing: Are you receiving positive buyer action?

2. Establish a priority list for skill improvement.

    ☐ Assign a numerical value for each identified area needing improvement, from 1 (most) to 10 (least).

3. Create an action plan for specific skill improvement.

    ☐ Select a specific skill that provides the greatest impact for sales growth.

    ☐ Initiate a specific timeframe for skill achievement.

    ☐ Establish skill-development objectives for each sales call.

4. Use each sales encounter as an opportunity to improve personal skill levels.

    ☐ Practice selected improvement area before each sales call.

    ☐ Focus on area of improvement during actual sales call (real live fire practice).

5. Accept honest critique (self and other) of performance after each sales encounter.

    ☐ After each sales encounter, ask yourself: "What did I do well?" "What areas do I need to continue to work on?"

    ☐ When working with others, ask them to critique your performance. Have an open mind. Remember, they viewed what transpired as an unbiased third—party observer.

    ☐ At the conclusion of a sales conversation, ask buyers for feedback, as they are the gatekeepers.

6. Take follow-up action as needed based on critique and feedback.

Whose Career Is It?

Who's responsible for your personal skill development?

Professional sales-seminar trainers indicate that only 10 to 15 percent of seminar attendees will learn, improve their skill level, and put to practice in the field what was taught.

WHAT'S YOUR DECISION?

LANDSCAPE RULE # 4
Set yourself apart from the competition.

LANDSCAPE RULE # 7
Mental Toolbox

LANDSCAPE RULE # 8
Obtaining selling skills is an individual responsibility.

ABOUT THE AUTHOR

This book was inspired by the author's personal desire to share a solid sales process with individuals entering the sales profession or for the veteran to re-examine basic sales fundamentals' for successful selling.

Warren Schoening has dedicated his entire career to self—improvement and the development of sales forces for regional, national, and Fortune 500 companies.

His career path, leading to executive sales management, started in the sales trenches at street-level as a route salesperson. With more than thirty years of firsthand sales knowledge, he brings exceptional insight to the sales process via his unique experience of working directly with corporate sales forces and independent broker networks.

He attended Palomar College and augmented his education with course studies at the University of Michigan, Cornell University, and Columbia University. A USMC Vietnam veteran (1966-1968), he was awarded the Purple Heart and Presidential Unit Citation. He is a member of the military service organizations Purple Heart and American Legion and is lifetime member of the VFW.

He lives in the suburbs of Tampa, Florida, with his wife, Karen.

www.ingramcontent.com/pod-product-compliance
Lightning Source LLC
Chambersburg PA
CBHW030819180526
45163CB00003B/1352